An Easter Hunt
for Jesus

An Easter Hunt for Jesus

The Treasure of Resurrection Sunday

KAROL HANSEN

ANOMALOS PUBLISHING HOUSE

CRANE

Anomalos Publishing House, Crane 65633
© 2008 by Karol Hansen
All rights reserved. Published 2008
Printed in the United States of America
08 1
ISBN-10: 0981764355 (paper)
EAN-13: 9780981764351 (paper)

Cover illustration and design by Steve Warner

All scripture quotes are from the King James Version.

A CIP catalog record for this book is available from
the Library of Congress.

To Amy Jens,
May you always keep your eyes and
heart fixed on Jesus!
…EVO, Mom

Why "An Easter Hunt for Jesus"?

An Easter Hunt for Jesus is meant to replace the hunt for eggs with a hunt for Jesus. This fun treasure search will help you and your children celebrate Easter by learning more about the life, death, and resurrection of Jesus Christ. It will help you make Christ the focal point of the celebration of Easter. *When thou saidst, Seek ye my face; my heart said unto thee, Thy face, LORD, will I seek* (Psalm 27:8, KJV).

This book begins with a fun poem/riddle that the child receives on Easter. Each verse gives a hint as to where to find each of the nine clues that are hidden in different locations. These clues are small pieces of paper that the parent cuts from the back of the book, rolls into scrolls, and ties with a ribbon. Each clue contains a question or two about the life, Last Supper, death, resurrection, or ascension of Jesus Christ. After the children have had the fun of seeking out all the hidden scrolls, they will unroll them, read each clue, and then go find the common household item that is referenced in the clue. Once the child has gathered all of the clues, the parent then shares from the book the applicable Bible verses for each clue. A thought-provoking question is asked at the end of each clue devotion. This treasure hunt is sure to be a fun, memorable, and God-honoring celebration of the resurrection of Jesus Christ.

Seek ye out of the book of the LORD, and read...

ISAIAH 34:16

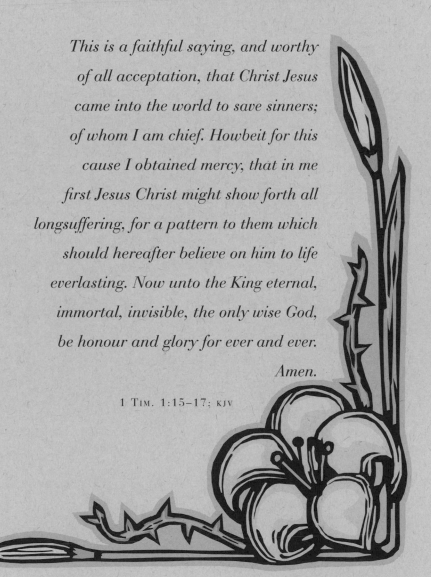

This is a faithful saying, and worthy of all acceptation, that Christ Jesus came into the world to save sinners; of whom I am chief. Howbeit for this cause I obtained mercy, that in me first Jesus Christ might show forth all longsuffering, for a pattern to them which should hereafter believe on him to life everlasting. Now unto the King eternal, immortal, invisible, the only wise God, be honour and glory for ever and ever. Amen.

1 Tim. 1:15–17; KJV

A Note from the Author

I, at first, thought my book would be staunchly anti-egg, but I have since revisited that thinking, and here is the reasoning:

Joshua 22:22, "The LORD alone is God!" This story in Joshua reminds us that things we do can be perceived as our action of building an altar for ourselves, for our own purposes in turning away from the LORD. This *An Easter Hunt for Jesus* book is for us to actively remind our children of our right to worship the LORD— especially in this day and age when that right is being taken away from us in the public square. In the face of efforts to take away our right to worship the LORD, either through unjust laws in the public square or through the colorful, candied commercialism of worship replacement that has us coveting candy-filled eggs, chasing bunnies or

celebrating Spring—celebrating a season instead
of the *Reason* for the season—this book couldn't
be more timely.

Though colored eggs and the origin of the name
of Easter have been argued to have their roots in
paganism—let's not forget that God made the egg.
There is a wonderful symbolism in the three parts
of the egg honoring the three parts of God: The
Father, the Son, and the Holy Spirit, so go ahead
and have some fun with eggs on Easter!

As for me and my household, we want to serve
the LORD and honor Him in our celebration.
God, very much so, has a "seek and ye shall find"
component to who He is, and I wanted children to
have the fun element of a treasure hunt—an active
exercise in God's "seek and ye shall find" in a God-
honoring way that exalts the relationship God wants
us to have with Him. He loves a mystery! And we
love being in the revelation of His mystery!

As we are shown in Joshua 22, it is good for us to have solid reminders of the relationship that we have with the LORD and the length to which He was willing to go to ensure us of that right. This Easter Hunt for Jesus is such a reminder, and a fun and active one, too! Joshua 22 is a good lesson for us not to build our own altars for our own purposes which turn us away from the LORD; but when we seek to honor Him and instill a reminder in our future generations of the relationship God created us to have with Him, I think He is well pleased and delighted.

May the LORD bless and delight you and your little ones as you actively seek and search for Him!

Because of Christ,

Karol

How to Conduct the Easter Hunt

While the children are still sleeping, hide their Easter treasure baskets somewhere way up high, then hide the clues in areas according to the riddle. Leave a copy of the riddle somewhere where the children are sure to see it before leaving their bedrooms. They can work together to find the same clue scrolls or work separately and each one gather the whole list of clues themselves (so, for however many children you have, you'll need that many sets of clue scrolls and clues if they're going to work separately). They may not untie the scrolls until they have found them all! Once the children have found all the clue scrolls gather them together in front of you and share with them that today they are going to learn about Jesus' crucifixion, resurrection, ascension and His soon return. Let them open one scroll at a time and read the clue, then send them to go and find that item and bring it back to you before moving on to the next clue until all items have been brought to you. Ask them to sort and put the clue scrolls and clues in order starting with clue #1. Now, begin to read each page in the book corresponding to the clues. Remember to take them to where their treasure baskets are when you reenact the disciples looking at Jesus' ascension so they will be sure to see their treasure when they look to Heaven.

A Happy

Easter Riddle

for Me

Sweet Diddle Diddle!

Gather all you find, but you shan't open any
'til you've found all nine!

When you get up from being a sleepy head, don't
    forget to look under your bed.
You never know what you'll find if you do...
    maybe a clue or two!

Walking as many large steps as you are old
    toward your bedroom door;
Turn, crouch down on your toes, sniff it out, and
    see what your nose knows!

Scurry and hurry to your breakfast plate;
You never know what awaits!

Finished eating, time to brush your teeth and
    brush your hair;
Hmmm, what have we here?

Time to get dressed before the morning chores.
Did you find something special in one of your
    drawers?

Now, I'm dressed, and I've only my shoes to don;
Which ones, which ones—only the ones with the
    something inside shall I put on!

Every morning Mother likes to get kissed;
What's that in her hair? Something I almost
    missed!

Into the car, quick as I go—here's a clue waiting
    for me; wouldn't ya know!

Last and final clue;
Bring me my Bible, please.
Rise and Shine, and give God the Glory;
Today you'll hear the World's Greatest Story.

Clue #1

A Lamb

The Bible calls Jesus the Lamb of God.

The next day John seeth Jesus coming unto him,
and saith, Behold the Lamb of God,
which taketh away the sin of the world.

JOHN 1:29; KING JAMES VERSION

And looking upon Jesus as he walked, he saith,
Behold the Lamb of God!

JOHN 1:36; KJV

But with the precious blood of Christ, as of a
lamb without blemish and without spot.

1 PET. 1:19; KJV

For in ancient times they sacrificed a lamb
to atone for the sins of man, but man's sins had
become so great God needed an everlasting atone-
ment to reconcile his children to Him once and for
all—Jesus Christ, the *willing* Lamb of God.

In the Passover tradition, families are to take
a lamb without blemish and bring him into their
home, play with him, name him, care for him, feed
him, and love him. Then they sacrifice the lamb to
atone for their sins. How is this tradition a reflec-
tion of Jesus? Jesus came to us as a baby. Born in
a stable, He was without blemish or sin. He lived
among us, suffered as we suffered, was tempted
as we are tempted and, yet, was without sin.
Jesus was the *willing* Lamb of God for us,
atoning for our sins once and for all.

Clue #2

Three Nails

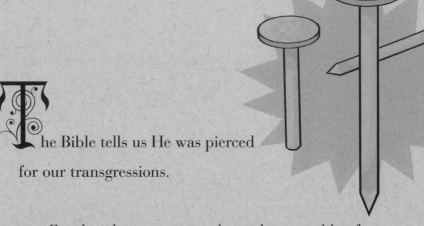

The Bible tells us He was pierced for our transgressions.

For dogs have compassed me: the assembly of the wicked have enclosed me: they pierced my hands and my feet. I may tell all my bones: they look and stare upon me. They part my garments among them, and cast lots upon my vesture.

Ps. 22:16–18; KJV

And I will pour upon the house of David, and upon the inhabitants of Jerusalem, the spirit of grace and of supplications: and they shall look upon me whom they have pierced, and they shall mourn for him, as one mourneth for his only son, and shall be in bitterness for him, as one that is in bitterness for his firstborn.

ZECH. 12:10; KJV

But one of the soldiers with a spear pierced his side, and forthwith came there out blood and water. And he that saw it bare record, and his record is true: and he knoweth that he saith true, that ye might believe. For these things were done, that the scripture should be fulfilled, A bone of him shall not be broken. And again another scripture saith, They shall look on him whom they pierced.

JOHN 19:34–37; KJV

Behold, he cometh with clouds; and every eye shall see him, and they also which pierced him: and all kindreds of the earth shall wail because of him. Even so, Amen.

REV. 1:7; KJV

Three nails—three crosses—three days until He was resurrected. What do you think God is signifying with using three so often? (Father, Son, and Holy Spirit.)

Clue #3

A Towel

Jesus says whoever wants to lead must learn how to serve, for no great leader can know how to lead without first knowing how to serve.

If any man serve me, let him follow me; and
where I am, there shall also my servant be:
if any man serve me, him will my Father honour.

JOHN 12:26; KJV

He riseth from supper, and laid aside his
garments; and took a towel, and girded himself.
After that he poureth water into a basin, and
began to wash the disciples' feet, and to wipe
them with the towel wherewith he was girded.

Then cometh he to Simon Peter: and Peter saith unto him, Lord, dost thou wash my feet? Jesus answered and said unto him, What I do thou knowest not now; but thou shalt know hereafter. Peter saith unto him, Thou shalt never wash my feet. Jesus answered him, If I wash thee not, thou hast no part with me.

JOHN 13:4–8; KJV

No man can serve two masters: for either he will hate the one, and love the other; or else he will hold to the one, and despise the other.
Ye cannot serve God and mammon. Therefore I say unto you, Take no thought for your life, what ye shall eat, or what ye

shall drink; nor yet for your body, what ye shall put on. Is not the life more than meat, and the body than raiment?

How did Jesus serve? You must be willing to go to your knees and be willing to put yourself at others feet and serve there with Him, and He will fill your heart, mind and soul like you've never known before! He will fill you to overflowing!

Clue #4

A
Meal/Food

Jesus dipped a piece of bread in the cup with his hand at the moment that another disciple did the same—it was only then that Jesus ever revealed His betrayer. In fact, when Jesus revealed that someone sitting at the table would betray Him, the disciples began saying, "Not I, Lord!" "Surely, not I Lord!" Until that moment, the other disciples never received any indication from the way Jesus treated Judas that he was anything other than loved; yet Jesus knew all along that Judas was His betrayer. Could we then also show no bitterness in our hearts toward those who have done or intend to do us wrong?

After Peter had denied Jesus three times, Jesus said: "Go and tell the others that I have risen from the dead and that I will meet them in Galilee"—*especially* Peter! In Galilee Jesus ate fish with Peter on the beach.

We often see Jesus blessing, healing, and pouring His love on others around a meal. The act of eating the fish with Peter shows He was resurrected from the dead and was real, alive, breathing, and eating. Some say Jesus wasn't really resurrected, that it was just a ghost of Jesus that people saw. But can you touch a ghost? Does a ghost eat? No. Jesus is RISEN! He's alive and just as He departed, ascending on clouds, He will come again!

Clue 5

A Hammer

Jesus was a carpenter. He used a hammer by trade to do His work. He could tell from the sound of the hammer hitting the nail whether it was being driven straight and true. What do you think about the fact that the tool that He used to make a living and that He was so skilled with would be the tool used to drive the nails through His hands and feet? Remember that God will use things in your life that are familiar and unfamiliar to do His work.

So the carpenter encouraged the goldsmith,

and he that smootheth with the hammer

him that smote the anvil, saying, It is ready

for the soldering: and he fastened it with

nails, that it should not be moved.

Isa. 41:7; KJV

Is not this the carpenter, the son of Mary, the

brother of James, and Joses, and of Juda, and

Simon? and are not his sisters here with us?

Mark 6:3; KJV

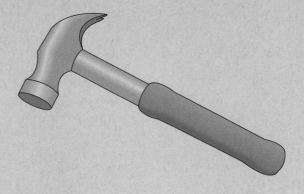

Clue #6

It's the Child Himself!

After Jesus was resurrected, He walked on this earth for more than 50 days and appeared to more than 500 people! He ate with His disciples. Thomas said he would not believe Jesus had risen from the dead until he could see Him for himself and touch His scars. Then eight days later, Jesus appeared in the room with the disciples. He came right into the room—he did not knock on the door, nor did he enter through the door.

The other disciples therefore said unto him,
We have seen the Lord. But he said unto them,
Except I shall see in his hands the print of the
nails, and put my finger into the print of the
nails, and thrust my hand into his side, I will
not believe. And after eight days again his
disciples were within, and Thomas with them:
then came Jesus, the doors being shut, and
stood in the midst, and said, Peace be unto
you. Then saith he to Thomas, Reach hither thy
finger, and behold my hands; and reach hither
thy hand, and thrust it into my side: and be not
faithless, but believing. And Thomas answered
and said unto him, My Lord and my God. Jesus
saith unto him, Thomas, because thou hast
seen me, thou hast believed: blessed are they
that have not seen, and yet have believed.

JOHN 20:25–29; KJV

What does it take to believe in Jesus? Can I believe in Jesus for you? Can someone else? It takes YOU!

Clue #7

The Bible

What do you need in order to know the will of God for your life? You need the Bible—in the open position with your eyes and mouth reading it. The Bible is the source of God's breath on this Earth. What happened when God breathed on Adam? He became alive. And so will you if you inhale God's Word—reading it and exhaling God's Word—saying it out loud, memorizing it, doing what it says to do.

But he answered and said, It is written, Man
shall not live by bread alone, but by every word
that proceedeth out of the mouth of God.

MATT. 4:4; KJV

And they were astonished at his doctrine:
for his word was with power.

LUKE 4:32; KJV

And he answered and said unto them,

My mother and my brethren are

these which hear the word of God, and do it.

LUKE 8:21; KJV

In the beginning was the Word, and the Word

was with God, and the Word was God.

JOHN 1:1; KJV

And the Word was made flesh,

and dwelt among us, (and we beheld his glory,

the glory as of the only begotten of the Father,)

full of grace and truth.

JOHN 1:14; KJV

Then said Jesus to those Jews which believed on

him, If ye continue in my word, then are ye my

disciples indeed; And ye shall know the truth,

and the truth shall make you free.

JOHN 8:31, 32; KJV

Clue #8

Praying Hands

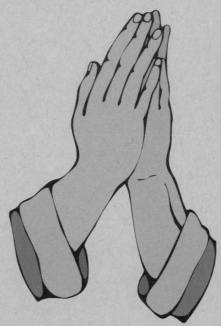

In John 15, Jesus says: "Abide in me, and I in you." How can we abide in Jesus? By praying. Listen to the rest of what Jesus says in this passage.

As the branch cannot bear fruit of itself, except it abide in the vine; no more can ye, except ye abide in me. I am the vine, ye are the branches: He that abideth in me, and I in him, the same bringeth forth much fruit: for without me ye can do nothing. If a man abide not in me, he is cast forth as a branch, and is withered; and men gather them, and cast them into the fire, and they are burned. If ye abide in me, and my words abide in you, ye shall ask what ye will, and it shall be done unto you. Herein is my Father glorified, that ye bear much fruit; so shall ye be my disciples. As the Father hath loved me, so have I loved you: continue ye in my love.

Here are some other important things that Jesus wants us to remember when praying.

But thou, when thou prayest, enter into thy closet, and when thou hast shut thy door, pray to thy Father which is in secret; and thy Father which seeth in secret shall reward thee openly. But when ye pray, use not vain repetitions, as the heathen do: for they think that they shall be heard for their much speaking. Be not ye therefore like unto them: for your Father knoweth what things ye have need of, before ye ask him. After this manner therefore pray ye: Our Father which art in heaven, Hallowed be thy name. Thy kingdom come. Thy will be done in earth, as it is in heaven. Give us this day our daily bread.

And forgive us our debts, as we forgive our

debtors. And lead us not into temptation, but

deliver us from evil: For thine is the kingdom,

and the power, and the glory, for ever. Amen.

MATT. 6:6–13; KJV

And when he had sent the multitudes away,

he went up into a mountain apart to pray: and

when the evening was come, he was there alone.

MATT.14:23; KJV

Then cometh Jesus with them unto a place called

Gethsemane, and saith unto the disciples, Sit ye

here, while I go and pray yonder. And he took

with him Peter and the two sons of Zebedee,

and began to be sorrowful and very heavy.

Then saith he unto them, My soul is exceeding

sorrowful, even unto death: tarry ye here, and

watch with me. And he went a little farther, and

fell on his face, and prayed, saying, O my Father,

if it be possible, let this cup pass from me:

nevertheless not as I will, but as thou wilt.

MATT. 26:36–39; KJV

Clue #9

Treasure
Basket

The Bible says Jesus Ascended to Heaven.

These things have I spoken unto you, being yet present with you. But the Comforter, which is the Holy Ghost, whom the Father will send in my name, he shall teach you all things, and bring all things to your remembrance, whatsoever I have said unto you. Peace I leave with you, my peace I give unto you: not as the world giveth, give I unto you. Let not your heart be troubled, neither let it be afraid. Ye have heard how I said unto you, I go away, and come again unto you. If ye loved me, ye would rejoice, because I said, I go unto the Father: for my Father is greater than I. And now I have told you before it come to pass, that, when it is come to pass, ye might believe.

JOHN 14:25–29; KJV

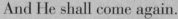

And it came to pass, while he blessed them, he was parted from them, and carried up into heaven.

LUKE 24:51; KJV

And He shall come again.

And then shall appear the sign of the Son of man in heaven: and then shall all the tribes of the earth mourn, and they shall see the Son of man coming in the clouds of heaven with power and great glory.

MATT. 24:30; KJV

And then shall they see the Son of man coming in the clouds with great power and glory.

MARK 13:26; KJV

Behold, he cometh with clouds; and every eye shall see him, and they also which pierced him: and all kindreds of the earth shall wail because of him. Even so, Amen.

REV. 1:7; KJV

I am Alpha and Omega, the beginning and the ending, saith the Lord, which is, and which was, and which is to come, the Almighty.

REV. 1:8; KJV

If we will keep our eyes fixed on Jesus in Heaven, He will lift us out of our Earthly troubles and make them not so big at all. When feeling down or in dismay, lift your eyes to the Heavens and scan the horizons for Jesus—God has a special blessing for those who are scanning the horizons for His return.

LUKE 12:37, 38; KJV

When we keep our eyes on Jesus we will find our treasure.

(Children will find their Easter Baskets hidden up high when they re-enact the disciples watching Jesus ascend to Heaven.)

Jesus' Command

If ye keep my commandments, ye shall abide in my love; even as I have kept my Father's commandments, and abide in his love. These things have I spoken unto you, that my joy might remain in you, and that your joy might be full.

This is my commandment, That ye love one another, as I have loved you. Greater love hath no man than this, that a man lay down his life for his friends. Ye are my friends, if ye do whatsoever I command you. Henceforth I call you not servants; for the servant knoweth not what his lord doeth: but I have called you friends; for all things that I have heard of my Father I have made known unto you. Ye have not chosen me, but I have chosen you, and ordained you, that ye should go and bring forth fruit, and that your fruit should remain: that whatsoever ye shall ask of the Father in my name, he may give it you. These things I command you, that ye love one another.

JOHN 15:10–17; KJV

Clue # 1

Jesus and His disciples ate this
at the Passover meal.

You have a stuffed animal like it.

Go and find it.

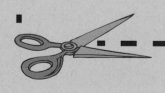

Clue # 2

They used these to

hold him to the cross.

Go and find three.

What were they?

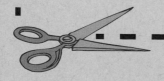

Clue # 3

He used this to do something
to the disciples the
night of the Passover.

He had to get on His knees to do it.

What did He do and what did He use.

Go and get one.

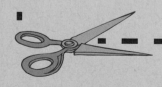

Clue # 4

His love was so great
that there was no malice in
Him toward those who loved Him
but did Him wrong.

What did He partake in
with two of His disciples?

Go and get some—anything that
is considered _____.

Clue # 5

What was Jesus?

Go and bring something He might have
used in order to do this work.

Clue # 6

Bring me what it takes to
believe in and submit to Jesus.

(Not the Bible because even Satan
knows the scriptures and doesn't
submit to Jesus.)

Clue # 7

Do you want to know the will of
God for your life?

Can I tell you what the will of
God is for your life?

Can Mommy or Daddy?

Bring me what it takes to know the
will of God in your life.

And what position must it be in?
(Opened or closed?)

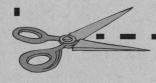

lue # 8

Jesus said, "For I can do nothing
without the Father."

Since His Father, God, was not on Earth
with Him, how could Jesus be with the
Father in order to do the things He did?

Go and find something that illustrates
what we are to do in order to stay
connected to God.

lue # 9

Jesus ascended into Heaven
with all of His disciples watching.

What would that have been like?

Pretend you are a disciple watching
Jesus ascend into Heaven.

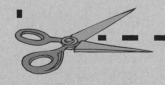

CLUE # 1

Jesus and His disciples ate this at the Passover
meal. You have a stuffed animal like it. Go and
find it.

_____

CLUE # 2

They used these to hold him to the cross. Go and
find three. What were they?

_____

CLUE # 3

He used this to do something to the disciples the
night of the Passover. He had to get on His knees
to do it. What did He do and what did He use.
Go and get one.

CLUE # 4

His love was so great that there was no malice in Him toward those who loved Him but did Him wrong. What did He partake in with two of His disciples? Go and get some—anything that is considered _____.

CLUE # 5

What was Jesus? Go and bring something He might have used in order to do this work.

CLUE # 6

Bring me what it takes to believe in and submit to Jesus. (Not the Bible because even Satan knows the scriptures and doesn't submit to Jesus.)

CLUE # 7

Do you want to know the will of God for your life? Can I tell you what the will of God is for your life? Can Mommy or Daddy? Bring me what it takes to know the will of God in your life. And what position must it be in? (Opened or closed?)

CLUE # 8

Jesus said, "For I can do nothing without the Father." Since His Father, God, was not on Earth with Him, how could Jesus be with the Father in order to do the things He did? Go and find something that illustrates what we are to do in order to stay connected to God.

CLUE # 9

Jesus ascended into Heaven with all of His disciples watching. What would that have been like? Pretend you are a disciple watching Jesus ascend into Heaven.